JOURNEY FRUIT

OTHER ALICE JAMES BOOKS
BY KINERETH GENSLER

Without Roof
ThreeSome Poems

JOURNEY FRUIT

Poems and a Memoir

Kinereth Gensler

ALICE JAMES BOOKS
Farmington, Maine

Library of Congress Cataloging-in-Publication Data
Gensler, Kinereth D.
Journey fruit : poems and a memoir / Kinereth Gensler.
p.   cm.
ISBN 1-882295-13-7
I. Title.
PS3557.E444J68   1997
811'.54—dc21   96-29647
                                            CIP

Cover painting by Mordechai Ardon, "Gilgal," 1965,
from a private collection, by permission of the owner.
Cover and book design by Elizabeth Knox, Boston, MA.
Printed by Thomson-Shore, Inc., Dexter, MI.
Author photograph by Miriam Goodman.

The text of this book is set in Sabon.

Alice James Books are published by
the Alice James Poetry Cooperative, Inc.
University of Maine at Farmington
98 Main Street, Farmington, ME 04938

ACKNOWLEDGMENTS

I am grateful to the editors of the following publications in which some of the poems in this collection have appeared, sometimes in earlier versions: *The Bridge,* "Overseas," "To Make an Offering; *Florida Review,* "The Last Parent;" *Passager,* "The Colony;" *Poetry,* "Birds," "December," "Writing Poetry;" *Radcliffe Quarterly,* "Elegy for Flute and Cello," "The Family;" *Slant,* "The Ajanta Caves;" *Sojourner,* "Bat Mitzvah: 1935," "Bowl with Pine Cones;" *Sou'wester,* "A Kind of Conversation," "Courage;" *Worcester Review,* "Escher's 'Three Worlds'," "April Poem," "Night Train to Vancouver."—With thanks to *The American Voice,* where "Hovering" and "Turning at the Coasts" appeared.

My heartfelt thanks to the friends who, over the years, helped to shape the manuscript, especially to Nina Nyhart, Ruth Whitman, Shirley Kaufman and Gail Pool. With ongoing gratitude to Kathi Aguero, Suzanne Berger, Erica Funkhouser, Celia Gilbert, Miriam Goodman, Helena Minton and Cornelia Veenendaal.

Alice James Books gratefully acknowledges support from the University of Maine at Farmington and the National Endowment for the Arts.

For my sister Avima Lombard

CONTENTS

To Make an Offering

❧ I ❧

❧ II ❧

CONTENTS CON'T.

❧ III ☙

To Make An Offering

Peel away the layers.
That's one way.

Or else, God's radical incision:
"Circumcise your heart that you may live."

But I shall let my heart be,
intact, as it was given,

removing only a plug,
—that test for ripeness—

lifted
as from a watermelon.

A plunge to the core
through the tough green casing.

❧ I ❧

Courage

Say a child dies. Yours.
And your second child. And the third.
And then your littlest one. We are not talking
about the end of the world, but yesterday,
in the time of the grandmothers,
my grandmother, for instance, whose children
died of tuberculosis in the old country.
Or it was the Black Plague.
Or influenza, in the 1918 epidemic.
Or children tossed on the tips of bayonets,
run through by swords, whenever,
Genghis Khan, the Ottoman Turks, the Nazis.
Because of the dead children, women cried at weddings,
knowing the young bride's future.
So where was light in the world?
And tell me, can there be courage
when there are no options?
My grandmother knew only:
you marry, you have children,
after the deaths you keep on going.
And of course you grieve, though some say
they would not let themselves care
for their little ones in the earliest years.
But my father, eldest son of her five new children,
was loved like a firstborn. Year after year

she made the choice: to love,
while grieving, each new infant,
knowing how frail its prospects.
That dappling in the world,
the recurring light.

Night Train to Vancouver

Home is en route, between places,
the train with its muffled voices
outside the stopped window—Kamloops
or some way-station. The wheels
turn and stop, stop and turn.
It is all one to you,
these movements in the dark
on the long crossing of the continent.
Riding high in the narrow berth,
enclosed by the green curtain, you rock
in the fluid place you knew
before thought arrived, or trust,
before you were hauled up screaming.
The wheels have their own rhythm.
In daylight, at a brief halting-place
you had a hushed view of wildflowers,
clumps of them growing tall and white
along the track in that hidden cut
of the western mountains.
                              You rock,
suspended, you give yourself over.
Never again, neither patient
nor impatient, will you follow a partner
as flawlessly as you follow
these starts and stoppings,
tucked in, the great
heartbeating engine all around you.

Overseas

Back then, before the United Nations,
before John Foster Dulles flew across time zones
with his instant airport-to-airport diplomacy,
to reach the Middle East you traveled abroad,
you went *overseas,* sailing on steamships,
one whole week across the Atlantic, and
from Gibraltar, gateway to the Mediterranean,
five days on small ships to the port of Jaffa.
Sometimes there'd be an overland journey:
the trains from French ports, Cherbourg,
Le Havre, the switching at Paris and, later,
train-to-boat transfers at Brindisi
or Trieste or Naples. Italy! All that geography.

At Port Said once, heading home, we boarded
a P & O packet, the *Chinwin,* out of Bombay,
bound for Southampton and laden
with Anglo-Indian wives and children, already weary
from the long passage from India.

In those weeks on board ship, a child would see
icebergs and dolphins and a churning wake.
You'd pitch and roll and were often seasick
but you knew with luck you'd get your sea legs,
a kind of balance, the agreement
a body makes with the humbling ocean.

You'd be out on deck then, playing with foreigners,
and swim in the sloshing saltwater pool
and eat, like them, at the early sitting
and learn a few of their words and habits.
People looked the same but were different.
Or they looked different but were the same.

What you learned as a child was:
you too are a foreigner,
speaking the difficult American language.
The need to pick your way, to go slowly.
How far the distance is between countries.

Driving

I imagine him sitting in the passenger's seat beside me—
my grandfather's father, a serf
on the estate of Pan Dobrodziej Kajeta
before Alexander II freed millions of serfs
from the land-owning gentry.
                 Buckle up, I tell him,
put on the harness, and he does. How adaptable he is,
thrown forward into a new world, a new century,
and this horseless *droshky*:
the speed of it, the powerful engine!
He grasps everything because he has imagined everything—
science, technology—,
the Bible having foreshadowed a sky with chariots,
this Jewish woodcutter, my pious ancestor,
who drives a cart piled high with logs
in a Polish forest.
            It's only me that he can't comprehend—
not because I'm the driver of this horseless carriage
but because a daughter of his family,
his own great-granddaughter, is bare-armed and bare-legged,
with her hair uncovered, like any peasant woman.

Bowl with Pine Cones

I fill my pockets with pine cones and empty them
in this bowl. Wherever I've been, I empty them.
The cones look alike.

Densely packed or open, large, small,
white pine or ponderosa, they look
more like each other than anything else—
the fruit, its seeds long gone, of the evergreens.

In the Maine woods, I rock in a hammock
slung between pine trees. My parents
lean against a white birch fence, watching.
They are very young.
They wear knickers and brown sweaters.
They look many-layered, lapped and overlapping.
I can tell they'll become
dry brown fruit, that they'll last.

Alexandria

The fat face of King Farouk, his red fez
on the postage stamps in Egypt;
pink flamingoes
strutting like odalisques in Farouk's gardens;

the shapeless body-searching woman at customs
poking her fingers
into my eleven-year-old body;
a man beckoning in the souk.

The flamingoes are gorgeous and grotesque;
maybe their beaks
have been tampered with, broken.
I find my father's hand and hold it tight.

Bat Mitzvah, 1935

Isaiah 54

Twelve years old, she was called
to the Torah—a girl, one of the first
to be what the boys were,
a child of the Covenant.
It was the end of summer
at the outdoor place of worship,
the Point, edge of the lake.
The congregation sat on benches
under the great oak tree with the Ark
carved high in the living wood,
its doors opening on the Scrolls of the Law.
She was wearing a white dress, afraid
the red stain might seep through.

Because she was menstruating,
an unclean woman,
they would not let her touch
the Scroll itself, so that this gift,
her rite of passage as a Jew,
became a withholding.
She read from a printed Bible,
chanting her portion from Isaiah: *Sing,
O barren one, who did not bear,*

break forth into singing and cry aloud,
you who have not been in travail...
be not confounded, for you will not
be put to shame.

Never would she lift the Torah
out of the Tree, unroll it and hold,
like a wand, the silver pointer
over its hand-lettered words.
Her portion, which seemed to promise
that she would not be put to shame,
was not about her—it was, as always,
about God and Israel.
And the Torah was not at the heart of the tree.
At the heart of the tree was the tree itself.

Freshman, 1939

She lived in the dorm with us,
a loud-mouthed rich girl whose daddy
was terra cotta king of the u.s.a.
We, too, came from someplace:
downstate Illinois, Chicago, Hawaii.
I came from Jerusalem.
She'd been to boarding school in Munich,
had a boyfriend in the German Air Force.
At the fraternity ball,
dressed as a popular song,
"I'm Stepping Out with a Memory Tonight,"
she wore a full-dress Nazi Luftwaffe uniform.

Such bad taste,
said the girls of Kelly Hall.
So horrid for her date.

In crowded bull sessions in the dormitory,
her subject was Jews:
how she could smell them in any crowd.
It was a sense one could develop.
Daddy's friend Goebbels had it.
Any Jews in this room?—
No, she said, checking us out.
The three Jews, with their bland faces
and unobtrusive pores, did not speak up.
By the time we graduated,
it made no difference.
In Munich, the ones like us had been identified.

Birds

It is because of the birds, beaked dinosaurs
flying around in my century, raucous and dirty

or obsequious, their falsely sweet trill-language
a trick to make me think that I could understand them—

it is because they could balance no-hands on air, go
places that I could not, unexpected as locusts

and as many—scavengers, indestructible,
a world presence preceding me everywhere—

and because I was schooled in genealogies, knowing how low,
like the reptiles, they had branched on the family tree—

and that, like spring, they came after winter,
with their bald beaks and swoop and fluttering—

and all of this before Hitchcock, whose film
confirmed what I as a girl already knew,

that I was right to hate them:
it is because of this that I understand prejudice.

Resisting Big Brother

after Orwell

A room, the Ministry of Love's Room 101,
all plumbing and no windows.
Grubs seethe in the drainpipes,
spiders mass on the ceiling.
At my feet, flies with torn-off wings
begin their slow climb.
The Marsh King waits
to suck me down with sewer beetles.
Big Brother knows—
he rigged this room for me,
he knows what's worst, he's watching.
My handcuffed mind slips sideways,
conjuring libraries:
Charlotte's Web, The First Books of Insects,
Darwin and the Beagle.
The room subsides.
Only the spiders stay, as they must,
in their natural corners.
I watch the one who squats above me.
She spins no words for me
but she's making something:
a line to reel herself back up on.
I watch her drop—that hairline plunge,
the light, retrievable body.

Center

at the hub of the wheel
the spokesperson
speaks for the farflung
circumferential ones
those who live on the edge
who keep running to make ends meet

down from the whirling rim
their words travel
losing by entropy
their little power
so that arriving
from great distances
they are almost exhausted

and the spokesperson
at the slow-moving center
is the receptor of faint messages
the focus
of our most desperate hopes

and the wheel is only one
of the wheels on the chariot

December

The cold comes indoors with the newspaper,
an exact reading of the weather outside
folded into its pockets, cold, chilled
like a foundling too long on the doorstep,
blue after battering, like an argument
for original sin, no newspaper without
its built-in dread, and the one
exceptional heartwarming story.
Cold shakes out from the creases
across the face, settling
at the body's mean temperature,
the smell of scorched food
pervading the whole house becomes
another odor domesticated, the smear of
fur and entrails on the highway is absorbed
by the wheels that keep passing over
and over it, and the newspaper turns
back into paper, our daily kindling.

The Family

We erupt from the past. The young ones
watch us, tell who we are:
great aunts, cousins-once-removed,
blood relations.
Thicker than water we cluster
in the snow-filled graveyard.

They watch our straight backs,
the clever hands they, too,
have inherited. They see
that we're crying.
What do they know of burials,
these young mourners?

We have come to show them.
Brittle as we are, we are the first
to throw handfuls of earth
into the open grave, onto the casket.
It is not impersonal.
We do not turn away. We peer
into their faces and say,
You look like your father.

Elegy for Flute and Cello

The Mishnah says,
     for funerals
two flutes and a wailing woman.
I say, one flute alone is enough
for the grief of a daughter.

Because your broad fingers
pressed the deep strings
and held them
and you bowed yourself over the chords
and listened
because it is winter
and ice shifts from the roof
I am shaken loose of an old confusion

The burden of perfection
     is lifted from me
the burden of rebellion
of wanting to be free of your music
your goodness   its tyranny
gone now like the absence of stale incense

I remember the wind of your walking.
It blows through me now as it did
when I followed your bier to the mountain.
When I was a small child and afraid

we walked in an open place and spoke
about dying.
     It was far away, you said,
and like cool water.

The Last Parent

The last parent gone—
and afterwards, orphan,
the sun's full glare is on you.
Unshielded by those large figures,
whoever you have become
is found out:
your irreversible sins of omission
the broken veins in your thighs,
your habits of refusal.
All the efforts to go lightly
have carved you:
a face as lined as theirs was.
You step out with short, flatfooted steps.
The ice—how it narrows your eyes. It shines.

Going to Jerusalem

It's a thing I keep doing
I keep going to Jerusalem though they said
take away your mother and your father
would you still come back?
I don't know I said then they said
now that your parents are buried
up there on the mountain
at the entrance to the city will you still
come back? I don't know I said
but like Jeremiah I yearned
for the wild iris in the fields the cyclamen
the ancient terraces of Judean sandstone
for the place of my lavish childhood
its armfuls of wildflowers freely picked
untouchable now, endangered species.
I am always returning. I keep these rooms
and watch the wide vista—the populated hills,
the Valley of the Cross, the Museum.
I come to this place with its carob tree and its garden,
my private leasehold
on whatever lives in these stony mountains.

Turning at the Coasts: a memoir

The **fellah** and his donkey, the donkey trotting along with gasoline cans filled with blood from the slaughterhouse strapped on either side, blood splashing on the road. Dry season, the blood a way of watering the crops. Because of the blood, my mother soaked fresh fruits and vegetables in potassium permanganate, a purple disinfectant, for hours and then washed it off carefully. There must have been nutrients in the blood as well as water, good nutrients as well as bad. Using everything the abattoir provided.

❧ ❧

In the 1930s, when I was growing up, my father had a winter job and a summer job. Winters, he was a professor of education at the Hebrew University in Jerusalem; summers, he and my mother ran a Jewish summer camp in Maine. Earlier, we lived in Chicago. We traveled enough so that I had whooping cough in Maine, measles on board ship, and scarlet fever in Jerusalem. Sea travel had its own slow rhythm, its own fascination, discomforts and boredom for a child who did part of her growing up on ships. There was the chance to meet people from the countries you would be traveling through, time to adapt to a new way of living, to whatever was coming.

Traveling on the margins of a continent soon to be engulfed by war, I saw Italian troops on their way to Ethiopia. I made friends with Dorit, a young German teenager who told me that her father was Jewish and her mother Aryan. She lived near Dachau and probably died in the concentration camp there. I danced with a German jewelry salesman who soon thereafter must have been drafted into the Wehrmacht. I was immersed every spring and fall in two different countries, different languages and alphabets, different smells: the Maine woods, Jaffa oranges. In between, the sharp Barcolene odor of ships' lavoratories. And then there was the deep kinesthetic sense of being *en route*, that pivoting of one's whole self, backwatering as ocean liners do when they turn at the coasts.

From 1935 to 1939 we lived in a part of Jerusalem called Talbieh, an Arab neighborhood. Those were the years of the Arab riots against the pre-World War II Jewish settlers of Palestine. No others Jews lived in Talbieh, as far as I knew; the only neighbors who visited were Lorna and Orde Wingate. He was a captain then; later he became General Wingate of Wingate's Raiders in Burma. Down at the foot of the street, to the right, was the lepers' colony. To the left of our house was an open square with a pillared mansion set back from it. Curfew nights, the neighborhood dogs would trot down the street and convene in the square, their barking the only sound because no cars were out except for an occasional British patrol wagon. Behind the house was a field of ancient olive trees— gone now, but owned then "in perpetuity" by the Russian Orthodox Church.

Our house in Talbieh was a Spanish Franciscan monastery called Montserrat. That was what my stationery said: Kinereth Dushkin, Montserrat House, Jerusalem, Palestine. The head of the Franciscan order, whom we called Père Ubach, another priest and a lay brother lived downstairs where they also had a room with an organ for Christian Arabs who came to pray on Sundays. My parents and Père Ubach spoke French with each other. To me and my sister he spoke in a Biblical Hebrew, something like, "Prithee, maiden…" We lived on the second floor, the apartment where young Franciscan priests had lived until it was decided that the Jewish girls walking around the city in their short shorts were too much of a temptation. The garden had lavender bushes and the fence had a vine, passion flowers, growing on it. Passion flowers are named for Jesus' passion because the flowers have a cross in the middle. I thought it was a good name, easy to remember.

I was a student at my father's high school. My bus stop was at the other end of the street, near Terra Sancta, the Italian school. Mornings, across from the bus stop, a slight man called The Negus would be standing in his rose garden. That was Haile Selassie, the deposed emperor of Ethiopia. He and his family arrived in Palestine by British gunboat when Mussolini invaded their country. On the day that Italian troops entered Ethiopia, the Banco de Roma in Jerusalem flew the Italian flag and declared a bank holiday for its employees in honor of Il Duce.

≈ ≈

On a bright desert day there can be darkness at noon. The train ride keeps returning, that ride through the Sinai Desert. We were traveling from Jaffa to Port Said; it was June, very hot. The train was a rattletrap left over from the first World War; it moved on a narrow-gauge track. My first and overwhelming memory is of the locusts blackening the train windows, smashing against them, the noise of millions of locust bodies. The windshield wipers up front, on the locomotive, must have had a hard time clearing a space for the engineer to see through. We were on our way to Egypt, traveling through a plague of locusts like the eighth plague that preceded darkness and the slaying of the first-born in the passage from the Haggadah that we read every Passover. Then the windows lightened, the locusts had passed, stripping everything in their path, and the train moved on with its smeared windows.

Before the locusts, an unsettling incident occurred. In the back of our railway carriage there was a closed compartment where veiled Moslem women sat in isolation. From it came a high-pitched wailing, the keening voice of a Kurdish woman. We learned eventually, through two stages of translators—Kurdish-to-Arabic, Arabic-to-English—that she and her husband were making the *hadj*, the once-in-a-lifetime pilgrimage to Mecca. Our last stop had coincided with one of the four times in the day prescribed for prayers, so her husband had gotten off the train with his prayer rug. The stop was not a scheduled one, it was only to take on water, and when the train left, the man was still praying in the desert. His wife was frantic, unable to communicate with the women in her compartment, to speak Arabic, to tell anyone what had happened. When a translator was finally found, the train authorities wired ahead. A lorry was sent back to collect the Kurd and his prayer rug from the spot where she had last seen him kneeling, facing Mecca.

✢ ✣

I was ten and a half. It was before the sulfa drugs and penicillin, when a child's only protection was vaccination against smallpox. I'd had practically all the childhood diseases and maybe I would remember the scarlet fever better if I hadn't started to menstruate. This was when we were living in Pension Friedman on King George Avenue in Jerusalem. I don't know about cause and effect, but first I had scarlet fever and then there were those brown stains in my pajamas. Menstruation is not a childhood disease, but I felt it was. Especially since I was in a room with a boy, Joseph. He must have been about eight. Neither of us particularly wanted to share a room, but at that time, in the Palestine of the British Mandate, our parents did not want to send us to the contagious diseases ward at Government Hospital. The alternative was to have our whole floor quarantined and to put the sick children in isolation. So there we were, on the top floor of the *pension*, with the shutters closed because scarlet fever can hurt your eyes.

At first, even my mother did not know what was happening; she herself had not menstruated until she was fourteen. But then there was the blood. The next thing was to get some sanitary equipment and teach me how to use it. Because of having a boy in the room, we had no mother-daughter talk about the wonders or curse of womanhood but just the nitty-gritty: in a country with no ready-made sanitary napkins, we had to roll our own. That meant buying lignin, a kind of cotton paper, in the pharmacy, and cutting strips from old sheets for rags. The idea was to make a neat little package, a wad of lignin wrapped in a clean rag, and put it between your legs and attach it to a sanitary belt. We practised in the w.c. To change the napkin, you would wrap the bloody filler in an old newspaper, put it in the wastebasket, and rinse out the rags and dry them.

Years later, I wondered what the girls in the concentration camps put inside their rags, and where they managed to rinse the rags out. In a way it was a relief to learn that soon they stopped menstruating.

❧ ❦

The four sister ships of the American Export Line—the Exeter, the Excalibur, the Excambion and the Exochorda— were small one-class ships, with no first class, tourist or third. I loved the way I could roam through an entire ship and not feel unwanted anywhere. And they sailed sometimes, all the way from New York to the eastern reaches of the Mediterranean without anyone needing to change ships to reach Palestine. After the war I asked around to see which of the Exes had survived the Nazi U-boats, but none of them had.

It was 2:00 A.M., early in September. We were proceeding to Naples through the Straits of Bonifacio, a narrow body of turbulent water between Corsica and Sardinia, and were asleep in our cabin when bells started ringing and the steward banged on our door. Lifeboat drill, only this one was real. Our parents opened the drawers of the upright steamer trunk and pulled out the warmest clothing for us that they could find, our snowsuits. All the lights were on in the corridors, people were tumbling out of their cabins, buttoning up; one Englishman, razor in hand, was shaving.

On deck, we stood near our lifeboat and waited, shivering. It was blowing and the waves were noisy. We could see a few lights from shore. Sailors started to lower our lifeboat and the winches creaked. More waiting. Then we were told to go back to bed. Who could go to sleep after almost being shipwrecked? My sister and I, ages eight and twelve, went into the lounge and played rummy with the purser till dawn. He gave us updated bulletins. First, that we had hit the uncharted wreckage of a ship; it ripped a large hole in the hold. Then, that by putting most of the ship's power into the pumps we could stay afloat and still make some slow forward motion. Further, the captain had decided that it would be too dangerous for small lifeboats to attempt landing at night on the rocky coast in such heavy weather. For a long time we heard the pumps working somewhere down below, in the engine room. Although the ship seemed barely to move, eventually we arrived in Naples. The ship had to go into drydock for repairs.

All the drydocks in Naples were in use when we pulled into port. Since our ship would have to wait its turn for a berth, the American Export Line put up the whole shipload of passengers at the Grand Hotel. As it turned out, we were there for a week. Naples is perched on a hillside overlooking the bay, a balancing of verticals and horizontals—city, hills and the flat stretching-away of water. I learned to love steep cities rising from the sea. Naples is where I read Dante. The Grand Hotel provided its guests with *The Divine Comedy* at their bedsides. Mine lay open at the Inferno—a beautiful volume with Italian and English on facing pages and a great many sepia drawings of the souls in hell, with interfacing sheets of transparent paper to keep the drawings from bleeding out into the text. From Naples there is a view of Mount Vesuvius. One can visit Pompeii, where a girl was caught by volcanic ash, sprawling, with her head on her arm. Where Lord Lytton wrote my then-favorite book, *The Last Days of Pompeii*, with its blind heroine, Ione (Ione was my mother's middle name). In the museum, one can still see tears stored in bottles, tears wept long ago by professional mourners. It was in Naples that I wrote in my five-year diary about walking with my father through the park in Naples, watching "lovers wrapped in each other's arms" at night. And it was there that my mind recorded indelibly the first young woman I saw, not a beggar, a woman like one I might become, unconcernedly breast-feeding her baby in a restaurant facing the bay.

❧ ☙

Chicago. I was small, so small I had no sister. We drove to the country to a place called The Social Workers Country Club. My father's driving was jerky and I was in the back seat, surrounded by suffocating plush upholstery: I threw up. He stopped the car and we all got out. We were standing on a side-walk next to an open field; across the street were stores. My father said, we're in Cicero, where Al Capone lives. My mother said, There's a drygoods store, we need to get her a clean dress, and she went across the street and came back with a new dress. From then on, I sat next to my father in the front seat and my mother sat in the back. At the country club, they sat at an outdoor table talking with their friends. I sat under some shrubbery and breathed in the flowers that grew under the bushes. Little white flowers and veined pink flowers: white hepatica and trailing arbutus. They smelled lovely, the opposite of vomit, a fresh flowery smell, and so wonderful to look at. I gave my doll a flower name: Bluebell.

❧ ❦

Wildflowers. In spring, at the end of the rainy season, I used to play hookey from high school with a few friends. We would cut school during English class to go climbing in the hills, picking flowers to bring home to our mothers. It was as though the entire countryside had bloomed in order to offer itself to us, the children, as though there were no end to what the land would freely give us. The hills, so full of stones, were suddenly luxuriant with red anemones, poppies and tulips, with narcissus and crocus, wild iris, cornflowers, sometimes the small speckled orchids. And always, growing in or near the clefts of the rocks, the delicate white cyclamen with lavender rims around their mouths. So many kinds of flowers, almost two thousand different species.

Those were the days when Jewish immigration to Palestine was rigidly controlled by the British government. World War II turned the ratio of people to flowers upside down. After the state of Israel was established and great numbers of Jews poured in from Europe and the Arab countries, temporary housing was erected everywhere, along the Mediterranean shore and in what had been open fields and hills. No one was prepared for the effects on the environment of such a sudden influx of people; streams were polluted, plant life trampled and uprooted.

When I arrived for my first visit after the war, in 1950, the Society for the Protection of Nature had already been formed and I discovered that a great many varieties of wildflowers had been declared endangered species. I could not believe that it was illegal to pick them or to transplant them. I thought that wildflowers were my own personal birthright. It was only then, I think, that I accepted as unalterable the overwhelming power of history.

✧ ✧

In March of 1939 my mother was in bed with amoebic dysentery. I have a photograph of her in the mahogany bed with pineapple posts surrounded by vases of flowers. One day Père Ubach came running upstairs, that frail old man with his wispy white hair and black cassock. He stood in the doorway of her bedroom with a bottle of his best wine in hand. Franco had won a great victory in Spain: Madrid had fallen to the Fascists, and he wanted to celebrate with her. Père Ubach was one of ten children, nine of whom were in the church in Spain, either priests or nuns, and all of them afraid of being killed by the godless Loyalists. What could my mother say? This was the war, the Spanish Civil War, we all knew would be followed by a greater war. There were German Jews already wandering around Jerusalem, asking for directions and I had learned a few words of German to tell them. He was a sweet old man. He was very fond of my mother and always prayed for her safety. What she finally said to him was: "I'm glad the war is over. I'm happy for you." In June, she opened camp on Lake George near Skowhegan, Maine. We were there on September 1 when Nazi troops marched into Poland.

❧ ❧

An orange is the perfect journey fruit. With its thick, faintly pitted skin and its slightly flattened poles like the earth seen from space, an orange is meant for the long haul, wrapped in a tough material that protects the thirst-quenching interior. Inside the outer casing, each segment of the orange is wrapped again in a papery membrane, like fine Swiss chocolates.

It was at recess in high school in Jerusalem that I first saw a pre-scored orange, a Jaffa, in the lunchbox of my friend Shoshana. Its thick skin was ready for peeling so that you did not need to claw into it with your fingernails. The way to score an orange is to mark a circle with the tip of a sharp knife in the skin around each polar cap, being careful not to cut so deeply that you touch the fruit. Then pull the blade down lightly between the two circles and make six or seven longitudinal slits around the orange. The strips of peel will lift off easily; the fruit inside remains intact.

The smell of oranges is the smell of my childhood. Orange groves grew everywhere in the lowlands and along the Mediterranean coast; oranges were the main agricultural export product. The groves were surrounded by hedges of cactus to keep out the goats. In the spring of 1937 I went with my class on an overnight trip from Jerusalem to the ancient ruins at Caesarea, Herod's old capital, on the coast. We carried canteens of water with us and olives, cheese, crackers, halvah and oranges. That night, we slept on the floor of an empty schoolhouse and sang patriotic love songs to the land. The next morning we were trailing our hands in the sea and stirring up the octopuses that lived close to the shore.

The teacher who accompanied us on that trip was Benvenisti, our geography teacher. He had come from Thessalonika in Greece, on the Aegean Sea. From him we learned a sea chanty in Hebrew that was a translation from the rhythmic working song of Greek sailors:

"The sea is calm, the waves are sleeping,
The sailors are singing songs;
The sailors are singing songs
And casting off the ropes."

Many of Thessalonika's Jews worked on the docks. When they fled to Palestine from the Nazis they became stevedores in the port of Haifa. Thirty-six years later, on a trip to Greece in 1973, my husband and I visited Thessalonika at the invitation of Christos, a former student of his. The fascist junta of the colonels was in power then, and on the plane from Athens we were ousted from our seats by two beefy men with gold teeth and government priorities. In Thessalonika, Christos took us to see—proudly, as one of the architectural sights—a new private dwelling. He pointed to the unusual stones incorporated in the wall surrounding the house; I made out Hebrew inscriptions: "Rachel, daughter of..." and other fragments from uprooted Jewish gravestones. We were speechless, his ignorance seemed so profound. Then I said, That's Hebrew, those are from gravestones. Oh yes, he said matter-of-factly, They're lying around all over the place, people use them for decorations.

I thought: he has no imagination, is that it? I thought: his feelings do not go beyond the people in his own immediate group. But I remembered Jerusalem, the layers of building stones uncovered from past centuries, how people have always used whatever materials are at hand to build their houses.

For one who is parched, eating an orange brings moisture back into a dry mouth. An unpeeled orange is faintly aromatic; when you rub it between your hands and breathe in, the orange groves return. But it is the odor of rotting oranges mixed with the odor of burning cactus thorns that is the old, triggering odor of home, the Palestine I grew up in: an odor from the groves at the edge of Arab villages.

In a Biblical Landscape

The Arabs say:
"When Allah sent His angel
to distribute stones in the world,
the sack broke over Jerusalem."

A riff of stones
from a slingshot: David's.

Catapult: rocks
shot against a Crusader tower.

Stoning: to throw stones at:
today's "children of stones."

Dudu, driving a milk truck
on his four A.M. route,
tucks a small pillow
between the side window and his head
when he drives past the stone-throwers
on the road to Hebron.

❧ ❧

The Five-Stone game,
a game for one hand:

Five small square stones
are thrown like jacks
into the courtyard.
Lift one, toss it up,
scoop a stone from the ground and catch
the one in the air as it's falling.
Repeat, scooping two,
scooping three.
Scoop four thrown stones,
catch the fifth as it's falling.
With your hand full of stones
flip all five
onto the backs of your splayed fingers.

Repeat.

❧ ❧

On the Day of Atonement,
remembering those who have died,
we recite the modes of death—
one is by stoning.

On the eve of Israel's election,
another reckoning:

The stone that Jacob used for a pillow,
where he dreamed of a ladder ascending to heaven
and set the stone up for a pillar
and named the dream place Beth-El.
And the stone he rolled from the well's mouth,
that brought him his bride.

Boundary stones, heaped,
gathered as landmarks between the tribes,
establishing a peace between them.

❧ ❧

The Psalmist says: "The stone
that the builders rejected
has become the chief corner-stone."

From riprap, gravel,
sand to fill the cracks,
building a highway in the desert.

❧ III ❧

in memory of Walter J. Gensler, 1917–1987

The Ajanta Caves

While you were lecturing—the distinguished
American professor of chemistry—and I
was waiting in the Institute's guest suite,
the courtly Director brought me
two rare volumes on the Ajanta Caves,
issued in the Britannic reign of Victoria
for the delectation of high officials,
with the choicest photographs of the frescoes.
I was turning the pages, beginning to enter
the exquisite sexual mysteries of India—
what page was my finger on when he came
back into the room and said not to worry,
they had phoned for the chief
cardiologist at Hyderabad Hospital
and a portable EKG machine and besides
you seemed to be rallying,
and I thought of Jackie Kennedy
as I walked the long hall to the auditorium
and there you were, laid out
on six narrow ladder-back chairs
intricately carved of dark mahogany
with red velvet seats, surrounded
by Indian students and professors,
and I said, Hello, and you said, Hello—
as though the caves had entered us,
shadowgraphs of the interior,
that quick flickering in our lives.

A Kind of Conversation

I

My fingernail,
bruised at the base
months after you died,
has grown out now.
Your chair, the one you rewebbed
is back in the yard again.
The kitchen paint job is holding up nicely
and I changed the door catch on a cabinet
with the short-handled Phillips screwdriver.

Of all the annuals Gail planted
after the funeral in a fury of planting,
putting color back into the earth,
a few snapdragons have returned
and some impatiens.
You would say as you said every May,
Why would anyone want to leave Boston.

II

I thought they were crazy,
the ones who talk to themselves
(I thought that's what they did), but maybe
they speak the way I speak with you,
who can't hear me, being dead,
asking you what to do (I know your answer,
after so many years, which helps),
catching you up on the news,
a not-quite one-sided conversation,
the habits of intercourse being so strong.

III

Time can be measured in miles. For example,
it's 12,361 miles since your death on my odometer,
and miles can be measured, or once could,
by the number of cigarettes it took to get there.
But I've quit smoking and you
never sat beside me in this new car saying,
as you did in the old days:
I was born to be chauffeured.

IV

The clock on your desk was there
through all of your comings and goings.
After your death it kept keeping time.
I was reluctant to disconnect it.
What did I think, that absence is only absence?
That you would return
as if from a sabbatical year away,
and I would be picking you up at the airport?
This is the long haul and we're in it.
In New England, the weighing stations
along the highways are closed.
But I will keep pulling off
onto a shoulder, testing:
is it heavier now? is it lighter?

Afterwards

Five years. No tour of duty lasts this long without a furlough. Not that I think you're alive, mind you, but it's hard to fathom such unremitting absence. Men have escaped from Devil's Island. Sometimes it seems you've opted for a monastic order. Last night I dreamed we met on Presentation Road in a motel room near the Pacific Ocean. You'd been studying law, you said, changing fields, and taking a course at the College of Jewish Studies. That was my father's college. You were loving, kind, remote. I understood you were dead.

Anniversary

I

Because you said, After six months people forget—
don't think you're not missed. You're missed,
much good though it does me. I want to tell you
that Judy came by with her new husband—
Judy, who showed up years ago with her Mafia boyfriend,
his drums, his truck, a dead bird and her two cats
and you gave them all supper. She buried the bird
under the appletree with the tire swing.
There's an empty space now where the tree was.

II

The oilstain in the garage
where your old vw stood
won't go away.

I remember that place on the peninsula—
the fallen trunks of ponderosa pine
springing with saplings
and us in our rain gear.
The mossy floor of the rain forest.

III

We had a 1940's marriage—marry a girl
young enough to admire you, don't marry
a boy your age who can't support you.
At 28, you were five years older.
Today we've come to a new anniversary:
I have outlived
the age you were when you died.

Hovering

I always knew that it was what he wanted, with his "Instrument of Anatomical Gift" to a Massachusetts Medical School signed fourteen years to the day before his death—the card in his wallet directing that his body be donated for "the purpose of transplantation, therapy, medical research or education." He was a scientist and a teacher. Approval by the next of kin was not required, but we did discuss it briefly, as husbands and wives do, in that high, abstract way one discusses the Big Bang theory and the distant end of the universe. For my husband, signing the card seemed a simple, sensible personal decision. I saw no reason to question it; in fact, I respected his clear-cut, noble wish to be of use even after his death, to teach as long as he could.

It seemed so improbable, impossible really, that either of us would actually die. We were in our vigorous early fifties and had just returned from a wonderful sabbatical year in California. Nothing in my experience prepared me for the effect of that Instrument of Anatomical Gift when, fourteen years later, at the age of seventy, my husband died quickly, within four days, of a cerebral hemorrhage. Directly following the funeral service, his body was whisked away to the medical school.

Five months after his death he was still unburied. What's left of his body, I thought, is tagged, stashed in the Medical School. Students, where do you keep your personal cadaver? It's hard for the next of kin to maintain objectivity. He's like Charlie on the MTA, never arriving at his destination and I'm the one who's riding a sleepless subway. I held his hand during his dying and his death so I know that the body, changing, becomes a corpse, turns wholly into matter. I understood, suddenly, an old belief, that the spirit hovers until the body is laid to rest.

This was not a simple organ donation, such as one signs for when applying for a driver's license. If he had donated his eyes or some other part of his body for immediate "harvesting" and transplant, we could have buried him within a few days, and gotten some comfort from that time-honored ritual. But he voluntarily gave all of himself, his entire body, to science, and science would only yield him up to the family when it was through with him. How could I fault him for that? But was I, too, required to be noble, to accept without murmur the thought of his dissected body? I thought of the difficulty medical researchers have always had in obtaining cadavers. I thought of the old Boris Karloff movies, of robbing graveyards, using the bodies of derelicts. And I thought of my husband, the body I knew so well, his strong arms cut open, the muscles taken apart for study by strangers—and I was immobilized emotionally, almost paralyzed.

How do you cope with having to live, month after month, with visions of dissected body parts? You keep your feelings on hold as best you can; you do time, like a prisoner. It helps to have a sense of humor: macabre humor, belly laughs from the hitherto unthinkable. For example, the day after my husband's death the funeral director told me that Boston University's medical school had its full complement of cadavers. He asked: "Do you mind if he goes to Harvard?" Aw sure, as they say in Minnesota, his birthplace, he can go to Harvard. Or, for example, someone from the hospital's intensive care unit gave the funeral director a wedding ring that had presumably come off my husband's hand. I slipped it on my own finger: cool in a crisis, that was me. Except that the ring had come off another man's hand, and his family was about to view the body in an open casket. Panicked, the funeral director phoned me. I realized then that we'd never had a double ring ceremony; also, that my husband's hands were large and that the ring fit my finger too snugly. I must have been hysterical with laughter or despair when I told the man to come and pick up the ring and added: "Tell them I kept it warm for him."

It was close to nine months after his death when my husband was finally buried. Although the medical school had released his body a few months earlier, the funeral home agreed to keep the remains until the spring when our children could come back again from their far-flung places for their father's burial service. At that point I learned more than I ever wanted to know about caskets: that the first one had been destroyed, in compliance with a state health law prohibiting the re-use of a casket. I needed to buy a second plain pine casket, a duplicate of the first, for the interment. Enough time had elapsed for a grandchild, who had not yet been born at the time of his grandfather's death, to be present as a babe-in-arms at the cemetery. Slowly, I was able to let go enough to grieve.

There's a belief we have that we own our own bodies, living and dead. I no longer believe it. The survivors, too, have rights: to the body, a casket, a wedding ring, something. Once, for a few months, when I was a young woman, my legs were paralyzed. When I recovered, I had acquired an abiding sense of kinship with all who are disabled. Since my husband's death, I have developed a similar sense of kinship with the families of missing men. With the wives of American soldiers missing in Vietnam. With the wives of New England seafaring men, walking back and forth on their widow's walks, uncertain, looking out to sea. We need something tangible to hold onto, and then to let go of.

Denial

There's always someone worse off
and so you are speechless, paralyzed
as in those months on the orthopedic ward
when nothing moved from the waist down
but the pain.
And afterward the slow recovery,

bargaining inch by inch with the unknown
(if only to sit, to stand, to walk),
the patience learned inside a hurt
so severe that I discovered
there can be pain
more protracted than childbirth.

How can you speak for your own pain
remembering the gurney rides to the rehab gym
and the door open
on children from the Burn Unit
dipped into the centrifuge,
their skin flaked off in that swirling water.

The years accumulate. It's no longer the pain,
but not to have spoken of it,
the learned pattern of denial, that is never over.

Scanning the Pavement

Mica sparkles under new crutch tips.
Hawkweed grows in cracks
where tree roots have lifted the sidewalk,
metal medallions marked WATER
are set in the slabs of concrete.

Shadows of fire hydrants and oak trees
lengthen. So too the shadow
of a walker on city streets shortens
and lengthens, but the driver of a car,
strapped in a rigid shell,

has no shadow. Upright and self-propelled,
a crutchwalker negotiates the earth,
managing treeroots and the curb,
that careful balance.

Writing Poetry

after William Stafford

It was lost for good, I thought, the writing, but no,
as the poet says and I quote, it is like a very faint star,
if you look straight at it you can't see it but
if you look a little to one side it is there.
It's that speck, the floater in my right eye
torn from the back of the retina and lodged
a little to the right of my vision. The particle
I kept trying to blink away and couldn't,
nothing but irreversible loss, damage,
until the eye became habituated, and I forgot.
Now, to bring it back I stare, unfocused,
into a middle distance. The speck floats,
steady as a planet.

The Law of Signs

When you need a sign, one will be given.
Anything becomes a sign,
even a fortune cookie,
that sweet sawdust.
The law arrives in a cocked hat,
white slip of a tongue
in the crooked mouth,
its words to be digested.
It will last long enough—
foretaste, taste, aftertaste—
to become addictive.
You will go through many fortunes
waiting for the perfect fit
between the sign you seek
and the written message.

Gilgal

for Mordechai Ardon

"When your children ask in time to come, What mean ye by
these stones, then say to them, because the waters of the Jordan
were cut off before the ark of covenant of the Lord when it
passed over the Jordan…"

Joshua IV, 6–7

These are bricks, not stones
that you have painted: a cairn of bricks
shining in the sun,
reminders of the bricks we'd made and set in mortar
for Pharaoh in Egypt but transformed,
these brick-stones, as if still damp
from their long sojourn in water.

It is moments after the crossing,
after the waters of the Jordan
stood up in one heap and we'd passed over,
dryshod as at the Red Sea,
into the Promised Land.

From the midst of Jordan,
the riverbed's dry center,
twelve stones were lifted,
hoisted one each on the shoulder
of the one man chosen from each tribe,
and carried across, into Canaan.

Joshua gathered the river-stones
into a pile and named the place Gilgal,
The Rolling, for the rolling-away
of the shame of slavery—
a memorial for this new generation,
born in the desert,
children who had never known Egypt.

Everything is new here, in your painting:
the stack of bricks,
each brick a different color—
even the sun is new,
red flecks of afterbirth scattered
in the glowing gold firmament.

Escher's "Three Worlds"

The shadows of three black trees
reach down in the water.
They stand on their branches,
rooted in their own reflections.
On the pond's surface, white leaves float
like maple and oak-shaped clouds.
The water is light and dark,
a thunderhead sky.

Under the leaves, so close
at first we can barely see it,
a great fish stares. The eyes bulge,
as in Escher's self-portrait.
The fish is a subterranean boulder,
hidden but unambiguous.
It is like the imagination, clothed
in scales and whiskers
with far-apart, straining eyes.

The Colony

By day a prairie—daisies and yarrow, shoulder-high loosestrife. We walk among meadowlarks, the small white cups of spurge and aromatic leaves of bergamot. Names still are a mystery. By night these acres are a field of fireflies.

At the edge of the woods, a path has been cleared, a single swath, one lane of mowing, hardly enough to disturb whoever nests in the grasses. Something like a train whistle hoots in the distance. Great care must be taken. The stars are more, and brighter. A run-off pipe lies buried among cattails and giant bluestems. A spring bubbles up through cracked limestone. Rabbits and woodchucks come.

At the time of the moon's eclipse we stood on a path of cleared meadow, white mist swirling a foot beyond us. The young people plunged and were ghosts. They returned clowning, shining torches on their upturned faces. The earth's benign shadow closed the moon slowly like a lizard's eyelid.

We have arrived by our separate conveyances but have much in common with each other. This may be the planet.

April Poem

Say you had long ago
stopped believing in absolutes
and distrusted truth,
beauty, religion, et cetera,
all things disembodied and immutable—
still the annual recurrence of wildflowers
is such a blazing field of particulars,
absolutely desirable,
that you are forced to reconsider everything.

Between One Life and Another

This is new for me
    watching the river
    doing nothing
       flowing
    changing as the river changes

Goodbye to the old house
    forty years
       it slips away

not lifted off its cellarhole
lost in a flood and drowned
    but stately
       like those houseboats
    that belong
       to somebody else

they come into view
    glinting or rain-drenched
as the single sculls do
and the long-oared racing crews
all boats moving
    past the river's bend
       on the moving water

It is distracting, this river
    you could watch all day
from the balcony
    the high windows

and forget where you came from:
    apples falling
    on the porch roof
before the hurricane took down
the last of the orchard's trees
    a baby crying next door—
not mine,
    go to sleep—
the dogwood sapling
and the long blossoms of wisteria
    under our window

Alone here, I watch the river
knowing the seasons in the garden
    what will wait
    what won't

The waves glisten
like the undersides of poplars
and raspberry leaves

On the Balcony

He stands on the high balcony dipping the loop of his wand into liquid soap and blows bubbles out over the railing into the autumn air. He is pushing his breath through flat wet circles. It is something to do outside, above the people down there, a good thing for a sad boy to make shimmering bubbles hang in the air and float. Why is the world unfair? Over and over he dips his wand into the glass jar. When the bubbles burst he blows another string of perfect globes. Then he's ready to go in.

for Josh

The Present

Sometimes I forget to breathe,
caught in time's crossfire.
Slings, arrows, they whiz by,
it's always the past becoming future.

Sometimes the air hovers in an earlier time zone,
charged with love and harsh cigarette breath,
where I'm always exhausted—babies, no money—
but at least I know who the good guys are.

I thought I could move freely across barriers,
bring everyone I cared for
into a continuous present, save them.
I cared for the whole world then,

a blue-green world I could encompass
with my arms, like the old schoolroom globe
that never changed its contours.
And no one I loved had died.

K I N E R E T H G E N S L E R grew up in Chicago and Jerusalem. She received her B.A. from the University of Chicago and her M.A. from Columbia University. She lives in Cambridge, Massachusetts and has taught in the Radcliffe Seminars for the past twenty years. In addition to her books of poetry with Alice James Books, she is co-author with Nina Nyhart of *The Poetry Connection*, a text for teaching poetry writing to children.

RECENT TITLES FROM ALICE JAMES BOOKS

Suzanne Matson, *Durable Goods*
Jean Valentine, *The River at Wolf*
David Williams, *Traveling Mercies*
Rita Gabis, *The Wild Field*
Deborah DeNicola, *Where Divinity Begins*
Richard McCann, *Ghost Letters*
Doug Anderson, *The Moon Reflected Fire*
Carol Potter, *Upside Down in the Dark*
Forrest Hamer, *Call and Response*
E.J. Miller Laino, *Girl Hurt*
Theodore Deppe, *The Wanderer King*
Robert Cording, *Heavy Grace*
Cynthia Huntington, *We Have Gone to the Beach*
Nora Mitchell, *Proofreading the Histories*
Ellen Watson, *We Live in Bodies*

Alice James Books has been publishing poetry since 1973. One of the few presses in the country that is run collectively, the cooperative selects manuscripts for publication through competitions. New authors become active member of the press participating in editorial and production activities. The press, which places an emphasis on publishing women poets, was named for Alice James, sister of William and Henry, whose gift for writing was ignored and whose fine journal did not appear in print until after her death.